UPSETTING
THE
WORLD

JOHN CROTTS

UPSETTING THE WORLD
Published by KRESS BIBLICAL RESOURCES
PO Box 132228
The Woodlands, TX 77393

Scripture quotations are from The Holy Bible, English
Standard Version, copyright © 2001 by Crossway Bibles, a
division of Good News Publishers. Used by Permission.

ISBN 978-1-934952-16-0

Cover design and typesetting by Greg Wright
(DiamondPointMedia.com)

Printed in the United States of America
2011—First Edition
10 9 8 7 6 5 4 3 2 1

Dedicated to my children:

Charissa
Danielle
Chloe
Josiah

May you upset your world!

Contents

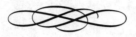

Following an Upsetting Man

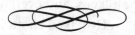

CHRISTIANITY WASN'T INTENDED to be a quiet religion. Faithful Christians aren't supposed to slink around in the shadows, just trying to keep to themselves.

I know you become nervous about beginning the conversation with an unsuspecting acquaintance. I know how tempting it is to leave out the hard parts of the gospel. I know it is easier to look the other way, when someone needs to hear about Jesus. But we were called to upset the world!

The Holy Spirit often uses vivid life examples to inspire and motivate his people. This book is a study of one such example. It is about Paul and his strategic evangelism in three cities: Thessalonica, Berea, and Athens. I intend to do more than just describe the historical scene. I hope to open your minds to the revolutionary methods and passion of the master evangelist, as seen in three distinct situations that closely resemble our own settings and opportunities. This is about you in your world.

As we trace Paul's path from ancient Macedonia south into Achaia (all of which is in modern Greece), we will encounter a passionate heart. Paul's zeal for the glory of God is contagious as he opens his mouth for Jesus in synagogues, marketplaces, and even among a gathering of elite philosophers. He talked about Jesus when people wanted to hear him and also when they were openly hostile to him. He experienced the pain of rejection, the sting of mockery, and the adrenaline rush of running for his life. He also experienced the joy of faithfulness to the Lord and the thrill of being used by God when others came to faith in Jesus. We can learn from people like Paul.

Joining in on a Journey

Paul's evangelistic ministry in the three cities of Macedonia and Achaia—Thessalonica, Berea, and Athens—is recorded by the inspired physician and historian, Luke, in Acts 17. These three encounters are a segment of Paul's second major missionary journey (Acts 15:36-18:22).

Before we arrive in Thessalonica, the first city in Acts 17, consider how Paul got there. The second journey began with Paul ministering over the familiar ground of southern and western cities of modern Turkey. Then, through a vision, God called him out of Asia and into Europe. Paul and his companions crossed the Aegean Sea into Macedonia. Once there, the team headed to the leading city and Roman colony, Philippi.

Luke describes three major events in Philippi in Acts 16. First, Paul preached by the riverside, resulting in the conversion of Lydia. Second, Paul cast the demons out of a fortune-telling slave girl. Her masters caused a great commotion because they were using her and her demons to make money. This resulted in Paul and Silas being imprisoned. The final event was the conversion of the Philippian jailer who heard the gospel from Paul and Silas following an earthquake that opened all of the prison doors.

After Paul was released from prison, he went southwest to a city named Thessalonica. This is where we will begin.

Thessalonica

Upsetting the Religious World

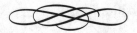

PAUL AND HIS COMPANIONS didn't arrive in Thessalonica freshly off of a Caribbean cruise. He hadn't just enjoyed a book-signing tour either. In his first letter to the church born during his time in Thessalonica, he wrote, "But though we had already suffered and been shamefully treated at Philippi, as you know, we had boldness in our God to declare to you the gospel of God in the midst of much conflict" (1 Thessalonians 2:2).

Paul, no doubt, stepped into the city of Thessalonica still stinging from the pain of the beatings and jail time in Philippi. In spite of the difficulty of the work in Philippi and the brewing opposition in Thessalonica, he boldly spoke up for Jesus once again.

Was the Holy Spirit extra-empowering, extra-illuminating, and extra-comforting to Paul so that his example is useless for regular Christians like you and me? Not at all. True, Paul was an apostle of Jesus. It may be that he had a fuller measure of the Holy Spirit's empowerment for ministry. When you see the ways he appealed for prayer from churches, however, it seems that Paul had a familiar sense of personal inadequacy. He begged the Ephesians to be "praying at all times in the Spirit, with all prayer and supplication."

> To that end keep alert with all perseverance,
> making supplication for all the saints, and
> also for me, that words may be given to me
> in opening my mouth boldly to proclaim
> the mystery of the gospel, for which I am an
> ambassador in chains, that I may declare it
> boldly, as I ought to speak. (Ephesians 6:18-20)

To the Colossians, he wrote that he was not ashamed to call for their intercession:

> Continue steadfastly in prayer, being watchful
> in it with thanksgiving. At the same time, pray
> also for us, that God may open to us a door for
> the word, to declare the mystery of Christ, on
> account of which I am in prison—that I may
> make it clear, which is how I ought to speak.
> (Colossians 4:2-4)

What about Paul's message? It is *the same good news* that you and I are charged to give in Christ's commission, which was first for the apostles and then for all believers to the end of the age (Matthew 28:18-20). Paul is highly motivated by the same gospel, the same charge, and the same resources that you and I share. He once said, "Be imitators of me, as I am of Christ" (1 Corinthians 11:1). His bold example amid great hostility to the gospel should encourage our weak hearts to action in our own spheres of life.

Paul's Strategy

Although it would be too simple to suggest that Paul had a surefire formula that he used to reach each new town for Jesus, Luke's record reveals a broad outline of common activities that certainly may be called a strategy. Paul didn't just happen to stumble upon a synagogue in Thessalonica—it was his custom to search them out (Acts 17:2). Church-planting strategist Jim Elliff has identified the main points of Paul's five-step approach in Thessalonica and the other cities he visited.[1]

1. Find the Synagogue.

> Now when they had passed through Amphipolis and Apollonia, they came to Thessalonica, where there was a synagogue of the Jews. (Acts 17:1)

Upon leaving Philippi, "Team Paul" used the great Roman highway, *Via Egnatia*, which linked Italy to Asia, leading southwest. Luke pointed out the main towns they passed through on their journey. Amphipolis was about 33 miles from Philippi. Apollonia was another 30 miles further up the highway. After another 35 miles, and no doubt several rest stops, they passed the "Welcome to Thessalonica" sign.

There is no record of any ministry in those towns on the way. He simply "passed through" them. This may have been because there was no synagogue in those towns, but the Bible doesn't give us the reasons. At least we can say these were merely stopovers en route to his main destination.

Thessalonica was the capital of the Roman province of Macedonia. It was an important city, right on the harbor at the head of the Thermatic Gulf. The *Via Egnatia* sent all of its access for trade straight through the city. Rome made Thessalonica a free city in 42 B.C., so it governed itself based on a Greek pattern more than a Roman one.[2] There were many gospel opportunities ahead for Paul and his friends.

The city had a significant enough male Jewish population for the Jews to form a synagogue. Paul found it and began to attend right away.

2. Reason from the Scriptures about Christ.

> And Paul went in, as was his custom, and on
> three Sabbath days he reasoned with them from
> the Scriptures, explaining and proving that it
> was necessary for the Christ to suffer and to rise
> from the dead, and saying, "This Jesus, whom I
> proclaim to you, is the Christ." (Acts 17:2, 3)

Jesus had also been a regular at the synagogue.
Luke reported that "he came to Nazareth, where he had
been brought up. And as was his custom, he went to
the synagogue on the Sabbath day, and he stood up to
read" (Luke 4:16).

The custom of Paul attending the synagogue and using
the opportunity for the gospel is well established by the
historical record. Here are just three of several instances:

> When they arrived at Salamis, they proclaimed
> the word of God in the synagogues of the Jews.
> And they had John to assist them. (Acts 13:5)

> . . . but they went on from Perga and came to
> Antioch in Pisidia. And on the Sabbath day they
> went into the synagogue and sat down. After
> the reading from the Law and the Prophets,
> the rulers of the synagogue sent a message to
> them, saying, "Brothers, if you have any word of
> encouragement for the people, say it." So Paul
> stood up, and motioning with his hand said . . .
> (Acts 13:14-16)

> The next Sabbath almost the whole city gathered
> to hear the word of the Lord. But when the Jews
> saw the crowds, they were filled with jealousy
> and began to contradict what was spoken by
> Paul, reviling him. (Acts 13:42, 43)[3]

For Paul, the synagogue was not simply a place to worship or to enjoy a little bit of familiar Jewish culture while traveling the Roman Empire. Rather, Paul was on mission. He visited the synagogues with the sole purpose of discussing the Scriptures in order to prove that Jesus was the Messiah the Jews anticipated. As we will see later, there is something in his pattern that we can apply.

Based on the content of the letters to the Thessalonians, it seems that Paul's stay, although relatively brief, was longer than just the three Sabbaths mentioned in Acts 17:2. He certainly worked in town long enough to leave a pattern others could imitate. "For you remember, brothers, our labor and toil: we worked night and day, that we might not be a burden to any of you, while we proclaimed to you the gospel of God" (1 Thessalonians 2:9). They were there long enough that leaders were tested and approved by Paul. "We ask you, brothers, to respect those who labor among you and are over you in the Lord and admonish you" (1 Thessalonians 5:12). In his letter back to the Philippians, he even mentions being in Thessalonica long enough to have received a gift from them (Philippians 4:16). Paul may have stayed in the city between 4 and 6 months.[4]

Initially, Paul enjoyed the opportunity the synagogue provided to reason with them from the Scriptures. The root of the term used for reasoning offers us the English word "dialogue." These likely were not Sabbath sermons as much as they were open discussions. This was not reasoning apart from the Scriptures, but reasoning flowing from the source of the Scriptures. These discussions probably involved taking a passage from the Greek version of the Old Testament and then exchanging ideas about its meaning, perhaps using questions and answers. The Jews had a ready acceptance of the authority of the Scriptures, so Paul likely read specific passages from their own scrolls or books.

Today some sections of the United States still have enough residual Christian culture from past eras that people retain a general knowledge of God, creation, sin, and even some of the basics of Jesus' life, death, and resurrection. It can feel natural pulling out a Bible in order to point out gospel truths as Paul was able to do in the synagogue of Thessalonica. Sadly, the problem in talking with nominal (or "so called") Christians is that they often assume a little knowledge of these Bible basics is all they need to be in a right relationship with God.

These residually Christian sections of American subculture, like those scattered elsewhere in the world, are quickly giving in to more pagan presuppositions such as Paul encountered in Athens. While Paul proclaimed biblical truths later in Athens as well as here in Thessalonica, he was not nearly as concerned in that non-Jewish setting to directly document his ideas as coming straight from the Scriptures.

It is often appropriate to give the gospel by summarizing the Bible rather than quoting chapter and verse, but Paul never models the use of man-made reasoning apart from Scripture—nor should we.

Paul explained and proved the necessity of Jesus' death and resurrection. To explain is to "open the meaning of something." Jesus, Paul's model and master, had done the same when he opened the meaning of the Scriptures to two disciples on the way to Emmaus. Those disciples were amazed at what they experienced. "Did not our hearts burn within us while he talked to us on the road, while he opened to us the Scriptures?'" (Luke 24:31, 32).

Paul's objective was to show these Jews that Jesus was the Christ that had been prophesied in their Scriptures (what we call the Old Testament). Seminary professor Sidney Greidanus once drove through a lush green valley in South Africa on his way to a scenic lake. He was completely astonished to return half an hour later to see the same valley covered with white flowers. He wondered if it could be the same place until he turned his head. When he looked back, the path was all green with only a few white traces. The flowers turned to face the sun. Driving to the east revealed only a few flowers, but when the car came back across the same valley all of the beautiful flowers were seen.[5] Your biblical vantage point also can determine the clarity of your understanding of Christ. Many of the misty predictions of the Messiah in the Old Testament became vivid only after their fulfillment in the first coming of Christ.

Paul sought to make his meaning very direct and clear just as Jesus had. To prove his point, Paul set what they already knew side by side with what he was trying to show them. The facts of the gospel are clearly rooted in the Old Testament. Paul surely highlighted the prophetic predictors which demonstrate how the Christ *must* die and rise again.

> For I delivered to you as of first importance
> what I also received: that Christ died for our
> sins in accordance with the Scriptures, that
> he was buried, that he was raised on the third
> day in accordance with the Scriptures, and
> that he appeared to Cephas, then to the twelve.
> (1 Corinthians 15:3-5)

The resurrection of the Messiah authenticated his perfect life and his sacrificial death. God set his seal of certification on Jesus by bringing him back to life. In those weeks of discussions Paul could have used several passages that indicate that the promised Messiah had to die and rise. Perhaps among them were prophecies written hundreds of years prior to Jesus coming, such as these:

> But he was wounded for our transgressions; he was crushed for our iniquities; upon him was the chastisement that brought us peace, and with his stripes we are healed. All we like sheep have gone astray; we have turned—every one—to his own way; and the Lord has laid on him the iniquity of us all...Out of the anguish of his soul he shall see and be satisfied; by his knowledge shall the righteous one, my servant, make many to be accounted righteous, and he shall bear their iniquities. Therefore I will divide him a portion with the many, and he shall divide the spoil with the strong, because he poured out his soul to death and was numbered with the transgressors; yet he bore the sin of many, and makes intercession for the transgressors. (Isaiah 53:5, 6, 11-12a)

> "The Lord your God will raise up for you a prophet like me from among you, from your brothers—it is to him you shall listen. (Deuteronomy 18:15)

> For you will not abandon my soul to Sheol, or let
> your holy one see corruption. (Psalm 16:10)

> I will tell of the decree: The Lord said to me,
> "You are my Son; today I have begotten you. Ask
> of me, and I will make the nations your heritage,
> and the ends of the earth your possession.
> (Psalm 2:7, 8)

After Paul established the Old Testament evidence for the mission of the Messiah, he sought to demonstrate that the historical account of Jesus' life, death and rising again corresponds to everything that the Old Testament anticipated. He sought to prove to them that the Jesus of history should be identified with the Christ of Scripture.[6]

You can imagine the shock that these Jews experienced as Paul claimed that the Messiah had to suffer and die. Jesus himself had prophesied many times about his death and resurrection, just like the earlier Old Testament prophets that the Jews had studied so carefully. Speaking of himself, he said, "The Son of Man must suffer many things and be rejected by the elders and chief priests and scribes, and be killed, and on the third day be raised" (Luke 9:22). Christ's death and resurrection had been revealed in the Old Testament Scriptures and in the words of Christ himself. It was *certain* to play out.

With those who accept and know the Bible already, and who are drawn by the Spirit, such an apologetic process makes sense.

After these weeks in the synagogue, a third part of Paul's strategy emerges.

3. Identify the Converts.

And some of them were persuaded and joined Paul and Silas, as did a great many of the devout Greeks and not a few of the leading women. (Acts 17:4)

Some of the faithful Jews who had been learning the Torah, planning for Passover, circumcising their sons, and spending their Saturdays in the synagogue, now believed that Jesus was their long-awaited Messiah. From a human perspective, had Paul and his friends bypassed Thessalonica, those ethnic Jews would have remained religious Jews. Instead of reveling in gospel light they would have stayed in the shadows.

These Jews were *persuaded*. In other words, they were convinced of the truth of Christianity. Their inward conviction was followed by an outward confession and an admission into the church.[7] The fact that they *joined* Paul and Silas probably indicates that they formed a group (i.e., a new church) that met separately from the synagogue, likely in Jason's house.[8]

In addition to the Jews that joined Paul, a great many devout Greek men and women did as well. The numerical difference stands out—*some* Jews versus *a great many* Greeks. These Gentiles may have been full converts to Judaism or just those that regularly attended the synagogue meetings. The women who came to Christ were apparently leaders in rank and social position. Most likely they were married to key citizens of the capital city. These Gentiles were listening carefully to the Old Testament Scriptures being read and taught in the synagogue. They were gaining knowledge of the one true God, though it was a shadowy knowledge. They needed to experience the bright light behind the shadows. When Paul brought the gospel to town, these few Jews, and many Gentile men and women, were illumined. Truth filled their minds as life-changing brilliance.

No specific numbers of converts are given, but the description reveals something of the mighty impact of the simple gospel discussed and proclaimed in the Macedonian capital. As many have observed, you have to sow in order to reap. Those converted to Christ were easily identified in contrast to the hostile backdrop of animosity that was forming against Paul and his message.

4. Face the Opposition.

> But the Jews were jealous, and taking some
> wicked men of the rabble, they formed a mob,
> set the city in an uproar, and attacked the house
> of Jason, seeking to bring them out to the crowd.
> And when they could not find them, they
> dragged Jason and some of the brothers before
> the city authorities, shouting, "These men who
> have turned the world upside down have come
> here also, and Jason has received them, and
> they are all acting against the decrees of Caesar,
> saying that there is another king, Jesus." And the
> people and the city authorities were disturbed
> when they heard these things. And when they
> had taken money as security from Jason and the
> rest, they let them go. (Acts 17:5-9)

The Thessalonian people pushed away from each other because of Paul's preaching; a raging division ensued. While it may seem like it is always a bad thing for groups to oppose the gospel, it can create some upshot. First, real Christians are easier to identify when the lines between following Christ and staying in Judaism or paganism are boldly drawn. Second, the gospel becomes more lucid to those watching on the outside.

The region of the southeastern United States, where I live, is commonly called the Bible Belt. A significant majority of people living in the region assume that they are Christians. Naturally, true believers do not stand out as starkly in that part of the country, nor does the gospel seem as radical as it actually is. Identifying true Christians and what it means to become one is less ambiguous in a context of opposition. Also, increased opportunities for the gospel can be another result of persecution. As the persecution grew in Thessalonica, these advantages occurred.

The motive of the opponents is revealed in the expression, "But the Jews were jealous." Can't you hear them complaining? "All of the Gentiles we have gathered to the synagogue are lining up behind this renegade rabbi Paul!"

In order to make their opposition work, the Jews needed to recruit some helpers. They dragged in "some wicked men of the rabble," or as the King James Version puts it so colorfully, "certain lewd fellows of the baser sort." Greek scholar A. T. Robertson succinctly called them "bums."[9] Basically the Jewish leaders found the bad boys of the marketplace in order to start a riot, hoping to have the missionaries arrested.

Apparently Paul was hosted by a man named Jason because his house was the target of the mob's violence. It seems reasonable to believe that Jason had come to faith in Christ. If Paul followed his pattern of seeking out the tentmakers for hospitality, like he does later with Aquila and Priscilla in Corinth (Acts 18:1-3), Jason may have been a tentmaker as well. Jason was a common Greek name Jews took when they joined the Dispersion to live in Gentile lands if they were named Joshua or Jesus.[10]

Luke tells us the mob wanted to force the Christians out to face the crowd. Since they couldn't find Paul, in frustration they settled for hauling Jason to the city officials. You can feel the intensity of the shouts of accusation reverberating through the narrow streets on the way to the forum. Their Christian reputation had preceded them.

"These men who have turned the world upside down have come here also." The point of this accusation, as John Stott notes, is that Christians and their message had caused societal upheaval.[11] They were agitators, stirring up unrest.[12] The word translated "world" is used for the inhabited world, which from the speakers' perspective was the entire Roman Empire. That sense of the word gives meaning to Caesar's command for "the whole world" to be registered (Luke 2:1), and the prophet Agabus's prediction of a famine to strike "the whole world" (Acts 11:28, 29). In a backhanded way, the wild Jewish accusations testify to the amazing impact of the gospel. After only a couple of decades since Jesus revealed himself alive from the dead to a handful of doubting disciples, the Roman Empire had been rocked by the reality of the proclamation of Jesus' resurrection.

Hospitable Jason is then blamed for harboring these troublemakers who are accused of preaching a rival king above Caesar. It was a very serious allegation. Noted New Testament scholar, F. F. Bruce said, "This was a subtle charge; even an unfounded suspicion of this kind was enough to ruin anyone against whom it was brought. In Paul's case there was enough smell of truth in their claim to make the charge deadly."[13]

What do you think Paul had been saying in the synagogues to draw this kind of accusation? He must have spoken of the kingdom of God and the Lordship of Christ. Perhaps he said that Jesus was "declared to be the Son of God in power according to the Spirit of holiness by his resurrection from the dead" (Romans 1:4); or, "If you confess with your mouth that Jesus is Lord and believe in your heart that God raised him from the dead, you will be saved" (Romans 10:9).

Paul didn't preach a fire insurance gospel by which sinners are called to mentally believe some facts about Jesus, merely adding him to their sinful lifestyle. Paul's gospel included a kingdom transfer, from Satan's kingdom to the kingdom of Christ (Colossians 1:13). Intentionally or not, the Jews perverted Paul's kingdom talk, originally meant to convey spiritual change, and made it appear that the believers were setting up a physical kingdom to rival Roman rule. It is easy to see how enough serious talk about Jesus as King and Lord could lead to this accusation.

The city officials took the charges into consideration but acted discreetly. Taking Jason's money was probably more than just a release on bail. Jason may have been forced to deposit a sum of cash that would be lost if any sequel to the day's civil disturbance occurred. He became responsible to keep the peace. This is what led to Paul and Silas being sent out of town, and maybe as well, seeing to it that they didn't return any time soon. Paul may have alluded to that circumstance in his later letter back to the Thessalonian believers, where he said, "We wanted to come to you—I, Paul, again and again—but Satan hindered us" (1 Thessalonians 2:18).[14]

Paul's exit provides the final part of his strategy.

5. Move on to the Next Place

> The brothers immediately sent Paul and Silas
> away by night to Berea . . . . (Acts 17:10a)

Even though Paul had to hurry out of town amid pressing persecution, he left part of his heart in the city.

There was a brand new church with precious new believers in Thessalonica. He was thrilled to see them continuing on in their faith.

> For this reason, when I could bear it no longer, I sent to learn about your faith, for fear that somehow the tempter had tempted you and our labor would be in vain. But now that Timothy has come to us from you, and has brought us the good news of your faith and love and reported that you always remember us kindly and long to see us, as we long to see you—for this reason, brothers, in all our distress and affliction we have been comforted about you through your faith. (1 Thessalonians 3:5-7)

How different is Paul's strategy than most of the well known evangelistic churches of our day? So many churches strategize as to how to get the largest crowd possible so that they can preach the gospel to them. There is a wide array of techniques used to gather a crowd. Older churches used buses and fun to bring kids to church. Contemporary innovations include elevating the entertainment value, modifying the messages to meet felt needs, pumping up the volume of the band, and adding to the drama. Emergent churches are becoming more mystical, giving post-moderns a place to meet without confrontation, where they may have a positive God experience.[15] Thankfully, some people are converted in these settings. Yet the gospel is often diluted or obscured through such techniques.

Paul, instead of planning a big event, went where the religious people were already meeting. Finding the synagogue, Paul took advantage of the open setting to reason from the Scriptures without gimmicks or entertainment, armed only with the gospel, the Spirit, and bold, sincere speaking. As he leaves Thessalonica, Paul keeps scattering gospel seeds. Faithfully scattering the seed, he joyfully anticipates the harvest.

How to Upset Your Religious World

Why is the account of Paul's adventures in Thessalonica in the Bible? At least one reason is to preserve Paul's example for future generations of believers. Many places in the world are saturated with religions other than Christianity. However, in the United States and in many other countries, many people think of themselves as believing in the same God and Bible we believe in, even when they don't understand the gospel at all. How can you make an impact on this massive religious segment of your society?

Recently a major TV preacher scheduled an event in a huge sports arena close to us. While this particular preacher is known for his big smile and a positive message, he intentionally leaves out the Bible's bad news of sin and judgment. I joined a few men from our church to engage attendees outside of the venue. We heard all kinds of replies to our basic gospel questions.

Though we had only a few moments with each one we encountered, we sought to ask one or two provocative questions like, "What is the best thing about being a Christian?" "Do you think of yourself as a good person?" "Can you define repentance?" or even, "How would you summarize the gospel in a minute or less?" Our hope was to sow gospel seeds and to provoke people to think about truths related to the gospel, as well as to distribute literature they could come back to later.

As person after person passed us on their way to listen to the preacher, they gave such weak answers to our questions that we had to conclude that most of them did not know Christ. Imagine thinking the best thing about being a Christian is loving yourself or working harder to live a good life! Even those that mentioned their sins being forgiven often had wide gaps in their understanding. We know that many such religious people need to hear the gospel. What are you willing to invest of your time and efforts to upset the religious world right around you?

Where else are the religious people gathering? Hundreds and even thousands attend Christian events like concerts and special days at theme parks. Many of these participants enjoy the sights and sounds of Christendom without loving Christ. Instead of assuming that they believe what their T-Shirts and jewelry proclaim, plan on arriving early to such an event to ask them. Bring along some evangelistic booklets that might be especially fitting for the occasion. Printing has become so affordable, you could even write your own tract and have a few hundred printed. It is surprisingly simple to hand a stranger something you have written.

Is there a coffee shop ministry hosted by a Christian group in your town? Many who come for coffee will of course need the Lord, but some of the hosts of such places are well meaning unbelievers themselves. Sincere efforts at religious activities do not earn a person salvation.

Where will the church people in your town eat this Sunday afternoon? The buffet restaurant near us is full of hungry religious mouths for several hours each Sunday. While they fill themselves with food, could there be an opportunity to address their hungry souls?

Have you ever volunteered to help out at a local Christian school? The organizers are usually eager to have someone interested in sharing an evangelistic devotional or a Christian testimony in chapel or a Bible class. Even the best Christian schools have non-Christians attending them.

I have been able to give talks from the Scriptures in a Christian-owned business meeting. While the owners knew the Lord, many of their employees did not. Or, how about visiting the local rescue mission?

Certainly bold efforts will be unsettling to some who are content with religion without Christ. I experienced push back from some I talked with outside of the preacher's arena. The shockwaves that Paul's efforts sent through Thessalonica were far more intense. For all the generations touched through the witness of the new church that gathered from those initial converts in Thessalonica, it was well worth it.

Berea

Upsetting the Inquiring World

PAUL WAS WHISKED OUT of Thessalonica by night. He and Silas traveled through to Berea, catching what sleep they required. While the events in Berea went quite differently than in Thessalonica, the five major points of Paul's strategy proved to be the same.

1. Find the Synagogue.

> The brothers immediately sent Paul and Silas
> away by night to Berea, and when they arrived
> they went into the Jewish synagogue. (Acts17:10)

"The brothers" of Thessalonica, who sent Paul on his way, were those brand new Christians that had come to Christ through Paul's remarkable time in that city. These brothers and sisters were those Jews, Gentiles, and prominent women who had been converted within about six month's time.

Using the cloak of the deep darkness of the ancient sky, the brothers slipped Paul and Silas out of town. Perhaps these new Christians were nervous about more mob violence, or perhaps Jason's bond may have required them to be removed from the city limits. Timothy is not mentioned until verse 14, so it is possible that he stayed behind to strengthen the young Thessalonian church family, while Paul and Silas, being the tallest lightning rods, scurried out of town.

Berea was about fifty miles southwest of Thessalonica. Even though they left at night, they would still have at least three more days walking before they arrived in this new town. Cicero described Berea as an "out-of-the-way town." By that he simply meant "off of the major trade route," the *Via Egnatia*.[16] Paul and his friends had been traveling the *Via Egnatia* since landing in Macedonia at Neapolis in Acts 16:11. Although they were now in a remote region, Berea would have been the most significant city in the area.[17]

Today's international traveling gurus often recommend going straight to the Traveler's Information post (TI) upon arriving in a new city. The kind workers at the TI usually speak a variety of languages, have maps of the city, and provide much helpful advice. Paul always had a different destination in mind—the synagogue. Paul wasn't looking for a map, or where to find a good Hebrew religious speaker, or where he could enjoy a Jewish worship service. Paul's mission was to share the Lord Jesus Christ and his resurrection with those in attendance.

Remember from where Paul had just come and what he had experienced there. Paul didn't wilt into self-pity or dwell on the painful drama of Thessalonica. He got right back to work. Paul had a compelling passion for God. His desire to speak up for God overcame any potential discouragement. How quickly do you bounce back if you get a negative reaction when you try to direct a conversation to Christ? When Paul experienced intense opposition or even a riot, he always got right back on the horse!

2. Proclaim Jesus.

> Now these Jews were more noble than those in Thessalonica; they received the word with all eagerness, examining the Scriptures daily to see if these things were so. (Acts 17:11)

The record states that the Bereans "received the word with all eagerness." What exactly does this mean? "Word" here is used for "message," meaning, "the message of the gospel." This message of Christ was based upon the infallible Scriptures expressed in their own words.

Paul also received what he longed for when he proclaimed the word. What occurred is a classic description of a well-disposed and open-minded response to the gospel.[18] Luke, in calling them "more noble," is making the point that those who are enthusiastic about the message of the Bible, who eagerly receive the gospel and then personally seek to verify it by comparing it with the rest of Scripture, are like nobility. The term originally meant "high born," but came to have a more general connotation of being open, tolerant, generous, or having the qualities that go with good breeding.[19]

Apparently, these Bereans enthusiastically listened to what Paul had to say. The idea behind the wording carries the concept of rushing forward.[20] They mentally "rushed forward" to understand more.

Consider the difference in the response of the two synagogues we have seen. In Thessalonica, the Jews heard the good news of Jesus on the Sabbath, whereas in Berea they wanted more explanation every day. These men and women couldn't wait until the next Saturday! While some in Thessalonica were persuaded of the truth of the gospel, the leading Jews were jealous and literally caused a riot to shut the messengers and their message down. The Bereans had no prejudicial rejection of the gospel; neither did they thoughtlessly and uncritically accept it.

The word translated "examining" (*anakrino*) was used of judicial investigations. Pilate *examined* Jesus thoroughly and judged that Jesus was not guilty of the charges against him (Luke 23:14, 15). Herod *examined* the guards when Peter was rescued from prison (Acts 12:19). Paul himself would later be *examined* by the Roman governor Felix (Acts 24:8). The marks of a good judge are integrity and a complete lack of bias.[21] Those qualities also marked the Bereans' investigation into the message of Paul. Luke intentionally highlights the contrast between the angry antagonists of Thessalonica with the careful reflective approach of the Bereans.

Ever since Luke recorded this account of the Berean reaction to Paul's message, "Berean" has become the moniker for those who diligently study the Scriptures before accepting something as true. The combination of receptivity and critical questioning from the Scriptures exemplifies the right response to encountering a new religious teaching. The Scriptures are the straightedge of truth by which every new teaching must be measured.

3. Identify the Converts

> Many of them therefore believed, with not a few
> Greek women of high standing as well as men.
> (Acts 17:12)

If Berea had a spiritual hospital, its maternity ward would have been overflowing! These spiritual midwives saw *many* men and women born again during the days that Paul and his friends worked there. The connecting word "therefore" ("therefore many of them believed," v. 12) links the new Christian converts with their in-depth examination of the Bible in verse 11.

Use the Bible in your evangelism. The Bible reveals the Creator to his creatures. The Spirit uses the Scriptures to convict sinners of their sins. The storyline of the Word of God points the readers to the Lord Jesus. It reveals his person and his work. You might be surprised how many people would be willing to do a four week Bible study with you. What if you just asked someone to read through the Gospel of Mark or John and then discuss their findings with you over lunch? Don't assume that such a study has to be formal, including blanks to fill in a booklet, in order to be effective! The gospel is pictured, portrayed, proved, and proclaimed all over the Bible! Get people to the Bible's main message and boldly expect the Holy Spirit to do his work through that message!

When Martin Luther was asked about the success of the Protestant Reformation he famously answered, "The Word did it all!" Sometimes evangelism begins as simply as getting God's truth to people and getting people to God's truth. The Holy Spirit delights in using the powerful gospel that the Bible proclaims to open the hearts of sinners. Don't be ashamed of the Bible. Don't be intimidated by those flaunting the latest greatest technique. Trust God. Trust the means that God has established to win sinners to himself—the gospel message of the Bible.

> So faith comes from hearing, and hearing through the word of Christ [i.e., the gospel message]. (Romans 10:17)

Amid such a powerful context of biblical examination of the gospel, there are still no guarantees that all will be saved. Yes, we need to sow seeds before we expect a harvest, but the Bible plainly teaches that not every seed bears fruit. There is reason to be confident in your evangelism, however, because the same God who loves to miraculously save sinners appointed the very means you are using.

Just as in Thessalonica, a division formed in Berea between those who received God's word and those who rejected Jesus. The groups that responded positively included Gentile men and women and many Jews, including prominent Macedonian women. From our perspective, it seems sad that this idyllic situation within the walls of the Berean synagogue didn't last forever. Not long after the divisions formed, those who rejected Jesus were gathered and mobilized, leading to the fourth part of Paul's strategy.

4. Face the Opposition.

> But when the Jews from Thessalonica learned
> that the word of God was proclaimed by Paul at
> Berea also, they came there too, agitating and
> stirring up the crowds. (Acts 17:13)

Until the Jews from Thessalonica came, it would seem that the unbelieving Jews of Berea had not yet become hostile or antagonistic toward Paul and Silas. These adversaries to the truth had been very successful in their agitating efforts back home, so they tried their strategy again. They attempted to recreate the circumstances that resulted in Paul's ejection from Thessalonica.

5. Move On to the Next Place.

> Then the brothers immediately sent Paul off
> on his way to the sea, but Silas and Timothy
> remained there. Those who conducted Paul
> brought him as far as Athens, and after receiving
> a command for Silas and Timothy to come
> to him as soon as possible, they departed.
> (Acts 17:14-15)

The brand new Berean Christians didn't wait for the crowds to become insane. They *immediately* sent the preacher out of town to the sea. Since Paul was the center of the attack, it was critical to get him out of the firestorm right away.

Paul's friend Silas, and maybe Timothy, left Thessalonica with Paul when he had to leave in a hurry (Timothy may have come later). In this case, however, Silas and Timothy stayed behind in Berea. The infant church needed nurturing, training, and the care that these faithful men could provide.

From the coast, Paul traveled some 150 miles south to Athens. It seems that he was conducted by some of his new Berean brothers in the Lord. They personally escorted him to Athens, all the while no doubt receiving masterful gospel training. Paul's final instruction was to have Timothy and Silas join him as soon as possible. Luke doesn't tell us when or how the pair reunited with him in Athens, but apparently they did make it. It seems that Paul then re-sent them to Macedonia (Philippi and Thessalonica). Following that, they rejoined Paul in the next major city of his journey, Corinth.

> Therefore when we could bear it no longer,
> we were willing to be left behind at Athens
> alone, and we sent Timothy, our brother and

God's coworker in the gospel of Christ, to
establish and exhort you in your faith, that
no one be moved by these afflictions. For you
yourselves know that we are destined for this.
For when we were with you, we kept telling you
beforehand that we were to suffer affliction,
just as it has come to pass, and just as you
know. For this reason, when I could bear it no
longer, I sent to learn about your faith, for fear
that somehow the tempter had tempted you
and our labor would be in vain. But now that
Timothy has come to us from you, and has
brought us the good news of your faith and
love and reported that you always remember us
kindly and long to see us, as we long to see you.
(1 Thessalonians 3:1-6)

When Silas and Timothy arrived from
Macedonia, Paul was occupied with the word,
testifying to the Jews that the Christ was Jesus.
(Acts 18:5)

How to Upset Your Inquiring World

In one sense, the biggest difference between the
religious Jews of Thessalonica and Berea was their
response to the gospel. The synagogue of Thessalonica
buzzed because of the message of Messiah that Paul and
his friends had brought to town. When the leaders saw the
eager response, however, they became jealous and hostile.

The noble Bereans, on the other hand, kept listening, searching the Scriptures, and believing the gospel, at least until the jealous Thessalonians arrived. The Spirit of God used the initial inquiring spirit of the religious Bereans to bring some of them to true faith in Jesus. Where should *we* look for religious inquirers?

Of course, there were no established churches in the cities Paul was visiting for the first time. Paul sought to engage the Jewish synagogues of his days with conversations from the Scriptures about Jesus. Perhaps liberal churches provide a contemporary parallel to the synagogues with whom Paul interacted. Although these churches often historically developed from the preaching of the gospel, those roots have long since died. The people who meet in these places expect to have religious conversations about God. While they generally recognize some value in the Bible, the majority of them do not understand its main message. Churches like these are far more likely to teach that a person becomes a Christian by their efforts to be good. They hardly mention Jesus except as an example to imitate.

What if you went to one of their Sunday School classes or Bible Studies and asked to participate? Even if you say up front that you are a part of another church, most liberal churches are so tolerant they welcome input from every possible source. It won't take long for people to recognize the difference between the comments from an evangelical believer based on the Bible and filled with Christ, and the ideas and opinions that usually bounce around the room. The striking authority of the gospel has often caused such groups to look to those visiting with biblical knowledge, sometimes even asking them to teach the class! Talk with your church leaders before attending another Sunday School class.

I took my wife to a liberal church's Sunday School class while on vacation in another state. It was almost shocking to hear all sorts of religious statements being added to the discussion soup. Some of the comments were actually orthodox, but many others were heretical. My wife tapped me on the leg a couple of times for fear I might participate too quickly. I waited until the very end of class. Even though I was a visitor, I asked if I could add something. The kind class assured me that I was a valuable part of the class, and that of course, I could participate. In a few short moments, I summarized the gospel as the ultimate answer to the questions that had been raised. The dozen or so others in the class seemed stunned. They thanked me for sharing, and then asked me to close in prayer! I prayed the gospel again. After the class, at least three class members asked if I would consider moving to the area to begin a church. All that response, and I had not told anyone that I was a pastor!

Christian bookstores are another potential haven for religious inquirers like the Bereans. Sadly, informal surveys have shown that most attendees of major Christian publishing conventions have little to no grasp of the true gospel. It is not only bookstore owners and managers that may be unconverted, but often patrons as well. These customers visit Christian bookstores for all kinds of reasons besides just purchasing Christian books and music. Many come in because of the positive atmosphere and to engage in friendly conversation with the employees and fellow customers. It's not unusual to find unbelievers in the Bible section.

Having worked for several years in Christian bookstores I have had countless conversations with dear saints of God as well as those who know nothing about their sins or the sufficient work of Christ. Be sensitive to the owners, but take advantage of the accessibility of religious people in a place where they expect to converse about Christian things. Ask them about their understanding of the cross. Find out what they have been learning from the Bible. Ask them about the changes that Christ has produced in them. Be aware of a few sound books on the shelves you could point them to, suggested by your conversation.

In the information age, religious inquirers are also to be found online. Are you involved in a social network? This can be an inexpensive way of cultivating gospel conversations with religious inquirers. Take great care with how much time you spend online and who you are chatting with. The devil enjoys enticing Christians into inappropriate relationships even if they are inspired by an evangelistic motive. As in all relationships, it is probably best for Christian men to refer inquiring ladies to Christian women for continuing dialogue.

Athens

Upsetting the Intellectual World

THERE IS ONE SMALL WORD in Acts 17:17 that answers the question of why you and I do not more often engage non-Christians. That word is "so."

"*So* he reasoned in the synagogues with the Jews and the devout persons, and in the marketplace everyday with those who happened to be there" (emphasis added). Paul energetically went to work engaging Jews and Greeks with the gospel of Christ in the synagogues. The rest of the day Paul invested in the marketplace challenging Athenians with the implications of one who was raised from the dead.

To those who have been in Sunday School, who have learned the stories of Paul, his ministry in Athens might not seem so remarkable. Remember, though, that Paul was a man of flesh and blood. In the space of a few months, he was ruthlessly beaten and imprisoned in Philippi, run out of Thessalonica due to rioting crowds of unbelievers, and forced to flee Berea before the next riot began. What could motivate such a battered man to open his mouth in Athens for Jesus?

The word "so," which begins verse 17, is a word like "therefore," grabbing something previously said and basing a conclusion upon it. Before verse 17 comes verse 16. "Now while Paul was waiting for them at Athens, his spirit was provoked within him as he saw that the city was full of idols." *He opened his mouth with the message of God because of his holy zeal for the glory of God.* His heart was a raging storm. Passion grew as he studied the city. In his speech later on, he makes mention of the fact that he had "passed along and observed the objects" of their worship (verse 23).

Paul took in his surroundings. As he examined the objects Athenians worshipped, he burned inside. Because he burned, he spoke. It is one thing to mouth the words in prayer, "Hallowed be your name," but it is another matter entirely to burn within when God's name is not being honored.

In those times when you don't open your mouth for Christ as the opportunity presents itself, could the reason be more vertical than horizontal? In other words, could it be more than not knowing how to begin the conversation, or not wanting to be embarrassed if they don't like what you say? Might it be that you lack zeal for the greatness and praiseworthiness of God?

Paul's Reaction to Athens

Paul, at this point, is alone in Athens. Soon Silas and Timothy would join their leader, but before they could get there the scene is set for a spiritual showdown. Here is, arguably, Christianity's greatest spokesman in the city known to have the most elite intellectual minds of the pagan world. Lightning is sure to strike.

The account of Paul's time in Athens is related in two main sections: (1) his intense interactions in the synagogue and marketplace, and on Mars Hill (Acts 17:16-22), which we will examine in this chapter, and (2) his major *message* in this Mecca of philosophy (Acts 17:22-34), which we will look at in the following chapter.

Idol Infestation!

Athens was in the Roman province of Achaia, which is the southern portion of modern Greece. Athens experienced its Golden Age in the fourth and fifth centuries before Christ. Philosophers Socrates and Plato were natives, but other influential thinkers such as Aristotle gladly adopted Athens as their hometown.[22] As a boy, Paul would have heard much about the great Athens, famous for half-a-millennia.

In the first century AD, Athens was declining, but still living off of its glorious past. The city still enjoyed the reputation of being Rome's intellectual and religious capital. Scholars from all over the ancient world went there to learn at its university. John Stott calls Athens "aesthetically magnificent and culturally sophisticated, but morally decadent and spiritually deceived, dead."[23]

Paul walked through the city like a tourist, seeing all of the sights. Looking up at the Acropolis he could see the amazing Parthenon. Athena's huge statue of gold and ivory had a gleaming spear point that could be seen 40 miles away! Paul was no uncultured barbarian. We might call him a graduate of universities in Tarsus and Jerusalem. He was a well-traveled Roman citizen. He probably had some enjoyment and fascination over all of the art, architecture, history, and wisdom dancing before his senses.[24] Unfortunately, the stunning artistry had serious religious significance. Any enjoyment Paul experienced was quickly overwhelmed by his knowledge of the evils of such idolatry.

The account says that the city was full of idols. In fact, it was *infested* with idols. One commentator estimated that Athens had 10,000 people and 30,000 idols![25] It would have been three times easier to meet an idol in Athens than a human being. Xenophon referred to Athens as "one great altar, one great sacrifice."[26] Idol statues of every kind and every size lined nearly every street. Pagan temples and their attending gods were everywhere. Paul will go on to describe the Athenians as, "very religious in all respects" (Acts 17:22).

Athenians were not suffering from a lack of sincere religion, but they were worshipping the wrong god. Sincere devotion to false gods leads to hell.

Stirred Up

What was going on inside of Paul as his eyes were assaulted by the array of idolatry? The inspired description was that "his spirit was provoked." Luke used a term from his medical background which contained connotations of a seizure or an epileptic fit. It came to mean "provoked," "angry," or "infuriated." Paul was not sinfully angry, but his spirit erupted with zeal for the glory of God. The tense of the verb indicates a continual action in the past, so this was not a violent explosive reaction, but more of a growing disposition.[27]

Henry Martyn, missionary to the Muslims of Persia said, "I could not endure existence if Jesus were not glorified; it would be hell to me if he were always . . . dishonored."[28]

Have you looked around your city lately? No doubt there is much to provoke you. God's glory is despised all around us everyday. Do you mind? Has your heart grown accustomed to these affronts? You will not rise to action until your heart begins to burn.

Open Your Mouth

It is in the context of this description of Paul's provocation that Luke, the author of our account, inserted the word "so." There would be no vacation from ministry while in Athens. Paul's heart ignited. He had to speak. Paul's experience paralleled the prophet Jeremiah who once said, "If I say, 'I will not mention him, or speak any more in his name,' there is in my heart as it were a burning fire shut up in my bones, and I am weary with holding it in, and I cannot" (Jeremiah 20:9).

With Paul, there was no helpless murmuring or wringing of his hands. Imprecatory mutterings to himself about the pagan Athenians didn't form on his lips. Retreating from the gospel in the name of separation was also not on the Apostle's agenda. Instead, he spoke.

Paul first employed his regular strategy of reasoning about the gospel with those in the synagogues as he had done in Thessalonica (v. 3) and in Berea (vv. 10, 11). He also opened his mouth in the marketplace. The *agora* was more than the local flea market with endless rows of shops. It also served double duty as the center of public life. The local temples, law courts, and town halls were found along the colonnaded porches which formed the heart of the city.[29]

Paul didn't rent a tent or put on a drama to draw a crowd. He just went where the people were. And he did so "every day with those who happened to be there" (v. 17).

Our marketplaces may be literal marketplaces. You could also go to a park, city square, coffee shop, street corner, mall, college campus, café, or club meeting. Go wherever there are people conversing. John Stott put it well, "There is a need for gifted evangelists who can make friends and gossip the gospel in such informal settings as these."[30] Can you make friends with the person nearest you in the coffee shop? Can you gossip some about Jesus? Give it a fresh try. Paul's faithfulness in small scale marketplace ministry would ultimately lead him to a much larger place to proclaim Christ.

Climbing up Mars Hill

No doubt Paul had many fascinating conversations with the Athenians and visitors during those days. Instead of relating each of them, the historian Luke selected the most significant gospel event for his record—Paul's address to the Areopagus (Mars Hill). Beginning with verse 18, Luke moves his readers towards that amazing account.

We've seen Paul wrestling with the leading rabbis in three different synagogues. But Paul is also not afraid to engage passersby or even pagan philosophers. In Athens, Paul encountered two pagan philosophical systems seeking to come to terms with the big issues of life:

> Some of the Epicurean and Stoic philosophers
> also conversed with him. And some said,
> "What does this babbler wish to say?" Others
> said, "He seems to be a preacher of foreign
> divinities"—because he was preaching Jesus and
> the resurrection. (Acts 17:19)

The Epicureans were founded by Epicurus (341-270 B.C.). They emphasized the importance of pleasure and tranquility. They sought to enjoy life detached from pain, passion, and fear.[31] Either there were no gods at all, or if they existed they were too detached to matter in the world's affairs to the Epicureans.[32] They taught that the world was just the result of random chance. There is no afterlife, and, of course, no judgment.

The Stoics were founded by Zeno (340-265 B.C.). Their name originated from the word *stoa* which denotes a colonnade, such as where Zeno taught. Zeno and his followers emphasized the importance of reason as the principle which structured the universe and men's lives.

Stoics stressed self-mastery in ethics, and indifference to pain or pleasure.[33] You are your own king, or even god! The version of god that the Stoics believed in was pantheistic. There is a spark of divinity in all people and all parts of nature.

Luke had important reasons for mentioning these two schools of thought. In his message to the Areopagus, Paul will directly address their beliefs, as we will learn. While each school had discovered some elements of truth, neither went far enough to have the whole truth, leading them to salvation.

The immediate surface results of Paul's work are recorded by Luke. They thought he was a babbler or just saying strange things. Those who called him a "babbler" were actually calling Paul a seed-picker. Literally that phrase was used of birds picking up scraps of food found in gutters. Figuratively, it came to be used of those who had picked up scraps of learning.[34] Here's a guy trying to pass off as profound what is really random scraps from the philosophical gutter! He is smoking used cigarette butts.[35]

Others just thought that Paul was weird. Socrates was accused of putting down the local gods of Athens and introducing new ones; apparently this was the Athenians' assessment of Paul. It is possible that the Athenians' use of the plural deities meant that they misunderstood the

Greek word *anastasis*, or resurrection, as a proper name for a second god besides Jesus. Just as easily, however, they could have been contemptuously dismissing the very idea of resurrection as taught by Paul.

After their initial reactions, some Athenians pulled Paul up to the center stage in Athens to check him and his message out more thoroughly.

> And they took him and brought him to the
> Areopagus, saying, "May we know what this
> new teaching is that you are presenting? For you
> bring some strange things to our ears. We wish to
> know therefore what these things mean." Now all
> the Athenians and the foreigners who lived there
> would spend their time in nothing except telling
> or hearing something new. (Acts 17:19-21)

The descriptive label Areopagus is a combination of two terms. *Ares* was the Greek god of war. The Latin name for *Ares* was *Mars*. *Pagus* was the Greek word for hill. Thus the Areopagus is also known as Mars Hill. Originally this was a meeting place of the scholars and leaders of Athens on a hill southwest of the Acropolis overlooking the Agora or marketplace. But the hill lent its name to the Court itself. In Paul's day, the Court also often met in the Royal Stoa or colonnade just by the Agora.[36] Just as Wall Street in New York City is a literal road but also shorthand for the American Stock Market, the Areopagus was a place, but also the title of the Court.

Under Roman rule, the court's power was greatly diminished, but in Paul's case it doesn't seem like a trial *per se*. There is no legal language, nor any record of a verdict being rendered. This was a public hearing of his views.[37]

Paul's strange teaching startled and surprised the Athenian scholars. This was different from their standard fare of dialogue and they wanted to understand it more thoroughly. Paul recognized this as a gift from God. This was an opportunity to clarify the gospel before the leading philosophers of a very significant city.

Luke tucks in a sarcastic side note about the Athenians sheer curiosity to hear something new. These guys had too much time on their hands! Ancient quotes show that the Athenians themselves admitted their passion for anything new could be carried to excess.[38]

If you share Christ with different audiences, you will undoubtedly find varying levels of receptivity. Paul's experience was no different. In Athens, there was a high receptivity to hear Paul's message, at least at first, but there was not nearly so much of a disposition to actually believe it. They just wanted to hear something novel. They didn't really care if it was true or if it applied to them. Stimulate my synapses, don't challenge my heart. Tragically, the Athenians didn't see themselves as spiritually lacking.

How to Upset Your Intellectual World

Put yourself in Paul's sandals as he follows these men to the Areopagus. What would you, the seed-picker, say when surrounded by the leading minds of the intellectual and religious capitol of the Roman Empire? Thirty-thousand pagan gods adorn the backdrop. Paul was an unlikely Jewish rabbi converted to Christianity, and yet here he was. You may never have the exact same surroundings, but you do have the same Savior who deserves to be spoken up for. Your friends and neighbors are not worshipping the true and living God. They don't really care about giving up their replacement gods and false philosophies, but God has put you there before them with an opportunity to speak. What are you going to do?

We'll study in the next chapter exactly what Paul said as God flung open the door to address the Athenian elites. Before we consider his content, let's be sure to capture his heart. The need for the gospel is as wide as the effects of the Fall; it is universal.

If you live near a large bookstore, have you noticed how vast the religious section has become? If you walk through the philosophy and other –*ology* sections you may discover quite an assortment of intellectual men and women to engage. Try to have a foundational question or two in mind to initiate the conversation. Asking a question about truth, ethics, or Jesus can alert you to the person's spiritual background and launch you into a helpful exchange. As we'll see, Paul's actual talk on the Areopagus is a superb model for proclaiming God to such people.

Bookstores and libraries often sponsor book discussions. If one does not already exist, why not volunteer to begin one? Even if the formal discussion doesn't make it all the way to the cross, the relationships you establish with the participants could lead to excellent follow-up opportunities.

Websites may allow you to reach out to intellectuals asking the fundamental questions of life. You could start a blog seeking to link God's answers to their questions. Perhaps, you could add a thoughtful reply to a post on an intellectual's blog.

Have you considered going back to school? Enrolling in a philosophy class at night could become a forum to bring the discussion to absolute truth. Just being on campus will also create other gospel opportunities with students and professors. How about posting a philosophical thesis on the bulletin board with your e-mail address and the message "Looking for Inquiry?" The wake of postmodernism has left an atmosphere on college campuses of openness to new thoughts. Every idea is fine except for Christian exclusivity. Although opposition to our message seems to be the one absolute truth, God uses the proclamation of that very message to open hearts, even the hearts of the intellectuals that are opposed to it. The fruits of Paul's labors in Athens are a source of encouragement to persevere in our efforts. As we will see, some believed!

Being able to write the gospel can be a useful tool in making you more precise in the ways you can communicate it to others. Intellectuals can be impacted by the gospel if you write an editorial for your local newspaper. Perhaps you could take a pressing issue in your community and create a bridge to God's ultimate solution. Even if you write a gospel letter to the editor you may be surprised by what makes it into print.

When Paul found himself surrounded by super smart skeptics of the Christian message, he did not back down. Nor should we.

A Message that Upsets the Intellectuals

P AUL HAD TAKEN IN the sights and sounds of Athens
for a few weeks. He had trampled through their
idol forest. He had engaged people in the synagogues,
the marketplace, and the city center. He knew the basic
beliefs of the philosophers of his day. Now he appears
on center stage, the Areopagus itself. As he opens
his mouth, he narrows his gaze onto the incredible
religiousness of Athens.

> So Paul, standing in the midst of the Areopagus,
> said: "Men of Athens, I perceive that in every
> way you are very religious. For as I passed along
> and observed the objects of your worship, I
> found also an altar with this inscription, 'To the
> unknown god.' What therefore you worship as
> unknown, this I proclaim to you. (Acts 17:22-23)

The assertion about being so religious could be taken
positively or negatively. The word "religion" has a wide

range of potential meaning. Positively, it can mean piety. Negatively, it can even signify things as dark as superstition or devil worship. As Paul began to speak, his hearers may have initially taken it as a compliment. As he continued to talk, his true opinion of the religiosity of Athens became apparent: Their rituals and philosophizing apart from God were empty and foolish.

The proof for Paul's assertion came from his observations about their objects of worship. One in particular caught his eye. He discovered an altar to an "unknown god." The very existence of such a thing is an amazing admission from proud, intellectual, sophisticated people. "I have no idea of the identity of this god that I am worshipping! I realize, at least a little, that I may not have all of the mysteries of life sorted out after all!"

Archeologists have failed to find an idol with that exact inscription ("To the unknown god") among the ruins of ancient Athens, but many ancient sources refer to similar inscriptions. A Greek traveler named Pausanius in A.D. 150 says that near Athens there were altars of gods both named and unnamed.[39]

Paul used this feature of their culture to present a right understanding of the one true God. Their admission of ignorance became the basis for his message, filling their empty minds with facts about the true and living God.[40]

Current events and cultural realities can be useful to change the course of a conversation to the things of God. What issues today might become bridges to a gospel conversation? Uncertain economic or political seasons can become a link to talk about the unshakeable kingdom of God. A new scientific discovery could be useful in pointing people to the creativity and power of the Creator. God's standards of right and wrong could emerge from a conversation beginning with a question of ethics at work. Any act of sacrifice calls to mind the ultimate sacrifice the Savior made for sinners. While we may not have the chance to customize a bridge about every issue, the discipline of intentionally forging a few of these cultural links will strengthen your skills in the midst of conversations about other issues.

There was no real connection between the Athenian idol shrine of ignorance and the real God. Paul's point was to emphasize the gaps in their religious knowledge. He is not giving credence to the errant idea that all religions are the same. The comparison Paul used as a launching pad for his gospel presentation was meant to address their ignorance only, not to validate their worship. He exposed the fact *that* they worshipped in ignorance, but said nothing that would affirm the idea that they were actually worshipping *the true God* in that ignorance.

Notice that Paul sets out to *proclaim* God, not to prove God to the Athenians. Everyone knows of God's existence in a limited sense because of creation and conscience (Romans 1:18-32). According to God's Word, even when people claim to be atheists or advocates of another religion, they are aware of the truth deep in their consciences—that God exists, that he has laws, and that he will judge his creatures. The degree of awareness is enough to condemn those who reject this general revelation, but not enough to save them. Pagans work hard to suppress those truths and worship substitute gods in the place of what they know. As you proclaim the truth about God, don't forget that you always have an ally found in your hearer's mind—his knowledge that God exists.

Paul seeks to fill in the gaps in the Athenians' understanding by proclaiming the big picture truths about God. The knowledge that people have from creation and conscience needs to be filled out with the gospel. The rest of Paul's talk moves his hearers to the essential elements of the gospel itself. Paul proclaimed God in five ways directing them away from their idolatry to the truth.

1. God Made and Rules Everything

> The God who made the world and everything in it, being Lord of heaven and earth, does not live in temples made by man. (Acts 17:24)

Directly opposing the Epicurean emphasis that gods either do not exist or have been removed from all relevance, Paul just says it! *God exists. God made you and everything else. God rules it all.* There is no dialogue about chance, random combinations of atoms, or matter being eternal. He just bends down and snatches the carpet out from under the Epicureans' feet with one hand.

With the other hand he grabs the carpet under the Stoics' sandals. As virtual pantheists, the Stoics worshipped their gods by worshipping creation. In contrast to their wrong ideas, Paul asserts that one God made all of creation—that God is not *in* creation; he is Lord *over* it.

Although the audience would not have known the sacred source of Paul's speech, his assertions were derived from the Old Testament.

> Thus says God, the Lord,
> who created the heavens and stretched them out,
> who spread out the earth and what comes from it,
> who gives breath to the people on it
> and spirit to those who walk in it . . . . (Isaiah 42:5)

> For in six days the Lord made heaven and earth,
> the sea, and all that is in them. (Exodus 20:11)

The problem with the evolution or creation debate is that sinful people don't come to the table with objective, unbiased minds. Sinful people don't *want* design or creation to be right because this would mean there is a

Creator. If there is a Creator, he will have something to say about the way his creatures are living. When one combines the inner witness of the scientist's conscience with what he or she already knows from observing God's creation, the truth possessed (or acquired through investigation) is significant and powerful. The only course left that will maintain such a person's sense of independence from the Creator, is to suppress that truth by giving preference to competing, though false, philosophies.

The men of Athens that Paul was addressing didn't believe in creation or a personal Creator. Paul knew that, but he also knew that the Athenians, underneath all their talk, were aware of those realities because of general revelation. So he tells them the truth they already knew but were suppressing.

Creation is a good starting point when you engage skeptics. Although most people say they don't believe in God as creator, internally they know better. Proving your points scientifically may be appropriate in some settings, but remember that you are not dealing with objective listeners. In most cases, follow Paul's example: Just tell the truth. Establishing God as the Creator and Lord is vital in showing someone their violation of his laws. When they recognize their guilt before the Creator of the world, they are much closer to acknowledging their need for a Savior.

This great God that Paul proclaims cannot be imprisoned in manmade structures. He who made and supervises everything doesn't dwell in boxes built by men.[41] Paul's words again leap forward from the Old Testament, although he did not quote from chapter and verse.

> But will God indeed dwell on the earth? Behold, heaven and the highest heaven cannot contain you; how much less this house that I have built! (1 Kings 8:27)

2. God Upholds the Universe.

> . . . nor is he served by human hands, as though he needed anything, since he himself gives to all mankind life and breath and everything. (Acts 17:25)

The folly of having to care for manmade gods is a regular theme of the Bible. The real God ridicules those who participate in such empty customs.

> A tree from the forest is cut down
> and worked with an axe by the hands of a craftsman.
> They decorate it with silver and gold;
> they fasten it with hammer and nails
> so that it cannot move.
> Their idols are like scarecrows in a cucumber field,
> and they cannot speak;
> they have to be carried,
> for they cannot walk.

> Do not be afraid of them,
> for they cannot do evil,
> neither is it in them to do good.
> (Jeremiah 10:3-5)

In contrast, for those who have needs, God is the source of all life.

> Hear, O my people, and I will speak;
> O Israel, I will testify against you.
> I am God, your God.
> Not for your sacrifices do I rebuke you;
> your burnt offerings are continually before me.
> I will not accept a bull from your house
> or goats from your folds.
> For every beast of the forest is mine,
> the cattle on a thousand hills.
> I know all the birds of the hills,
> and all that moves in the field is mine.
> If I were hungry, I would not tell you,
> for the world and its fullness are mine.
> Do I eat the flesh of bulls
> or drink the blood of goats?
> Offer to God a sacrifice of thanksgiving,
> and perform your vows to the Most High,
> and call upon me in the day of trouble;
> I will deliver you, and you shall glorify me.
> (Psalm 50:7-15)

Today people domesticate God in their own minds. While they don't try to fashion images of him out of chunks of trees, just ask people what they think God's role is in current affairs. Answers such as, "My God would never allow such a tragedy," "That situation makes God cry too," or that "God didn't have the power to stop the suffering," fills the hearts of many in our day. Is not our generation as equally guilty of manufacturing gods as Athens?

Paul made fearless assertions against the views of his hearers who believed gods to be distant and apathetic toward their affairs. "God," proclaimed Paul, "is actively giving you your life and breath while you sit here before me!" To those who believed that there was a spark of divinity in everything, Paul countered that the living God is both separate from, and the sustainer of, his creation.

3. God is the Lord of the Nations

> And he made from one man every nation
> of mankind to live on all the face of the
> earth, having determined allotted periods
> and the boundaries of their dwelling place,
> that they should seek God, in the hope
> that they might feel their way toward
> him and find him. Yet he is actually not
> far from each one of us, for "In him we
> live and move and have our being."
> (Acts 17:26-28a)

All people ultimately find their source in the original person, Adam. The Athenians believed their ancestors literally sprang from Greek soil. Like Jews, who viewed the world as consisting of Jews and Gentiles, Athenians separated the world into Greeks and Barbarians. If, as Paul stated, the same God made all the nations from one man, the Athenians would have to swallow a huge lump of pride. It was as if Paul was saying, "You and the Barbarians are related. You are no better and no different than they are."[43]

No matter the hair color, skin tone, or any other physical features, humanity all came from *one* God through *one* man and *one* woman. As you seek to faithfully proclaim the message of reconciliation of sinful people to a holy God, never do it with a sense of superiority over any other person. All people were made by God through Adam; all people fell into sin in Adam; all people need salvation through the last Adam, Jesus Christ.

Not only did all the people of the earth originate with God, so did the various times, seasons, and boundaries of every group of people throughout history. This seems to emphasize that God appointed periods for individual nations to flourish.[44]

God is even the one who determines every boundary line of every nation on the planet. This fact was set to music all the way back to the Song of Moses in Deuteronomy 32:8, "When the Most High gave to the nations their inheritance, when he divided mankind, he fixed the borders of the peoples according to the number of the sons of God." Certainly it has seemed like some of those lines have shifted back and forth over the years. God knows and controls even those movements. Every tyrant that has ever tried to gain control over the nations has been ultimately established by God. Ages before the United Nations was constituted, God determined every border of every country and empire that would ever draw lines on a map. This was true about ancient Greece, whether the Athenians knew it or not! God's sovereign lordship extends throughout all of history.[45]

The gospel is no mere tribal message from a small sect in the Middle East. It is global good news from the cosmic God. God's purpose in arranging the times and places for man's well being is "that they should seek God, in the hope that they might feel their way toward him and find him" (Acts 17:27).

All general revelation makes humanity responsible to seek God. God proclaims the truth about himself through creation and people's consciences, graciously provides for people's physical needs, and even separates them into nations with boundaries. Accordingly, the creature should seek the Creator. This drumbeat is heard throughout the Bible's storyline.

Seek the Lord while he may be found; call upon him while he is near. (Isaiah 55:6)

The Lord looks down from heaven on the children of man, to see if there are any who understand, who seek after God. (Psalm 14:2)

You will seek me and find me, when you seek me with all your heart. (Jeremiah 29:13)

"Ask, and it will be given to you; seek, and you will find; knock, and it will be opened to you. (Matthew 7:7)

People feeling their way to God is like looking for a hidden object in a dark room, or a clinically blind man fumbling around trying to find his glasses. In an indirect way, Paul is saying that the Athenians have *failed* in their search for God. As creatures made in God's image, we know God exists. Because of the Fall, however, we want our sin more than we want to arrive at the truth about God. We distort God's revealed truth, suppressing it as deeply as we can. We worship creatures rather than the Creator (Romans 1:20ff.).

As you seek to engage unbelievers, God's general revelation about himself is a great place to begin.

Paul continues by encouraging the Athenians that the one true God is "not far from each one of us." It is not God's fault that people are separated from him, groping around in the dark. He is not distant, unknowable, nor uninterested.[46] When it comes to God, ignorance is no excuse. Paul nails down his point with a powerful quote from Epimanides of Cnossos in Crete: "In him we live and move and have our being" (Acts 17:28a). Lifting this idea from its pagan framework, Paul uses it to make a spiritual point. Paul quotes this same poem in Titus 1:12, where he says, "One of the Cretans, a prophet of their own, said, 'Cretans are always liars, evil beasts, lazy gluttons.'" There are plenty of opportunities for us to borrow one-liners from culture to make spiritual points with people. Paul built bridges to connect with his hearers. In 1 Corinthians 9:19 he says, "For though I am free from all, I have made myself a servant to all, that I might win more of them."

Jesus regularly placed familiar concepts alongside unfamiliar spiritual truths in his parables. He used fresh stories about planting fields, fishing, keeping vineyards, buying real estate, treasure hunting, and even baking, to teach vital spiritual lessons.

A word of caution should be offered here. Sometimes Paul's methodology has been used to encourage people to dive deeply into the dangerous waters of contemporary culture in order to learn how unchurched people think. While it is our responsibility to speak God's eternal words of truth in ways our hearers can understand, the world is a dangerous place. There's a reason for John's warning, "Do not love the world or the things in the world. If anyone loves the world, the love of the Father is not in him" (1 John 2:15). Jude describes frontline evangelism in fearful language: "Save others by snatching them out of the fire; to others show mercy with fear, hating even the garment stained by the flesh" (Jude 23). When you engage people on the fringes of hell be careful not to get singed! In your efforts to surf through the world in order to come up with language and ideas non-Christians can connect with, you must always be on guard against the undertow of the evil one.

Is the ancient quotation just mentioned, and the one that follows it in the second half of verse 28 ("In him we live and move and have our being," and, "for we are indeed his offspring") as ultra-relevant as some have made them out to be? I realize that Paul was pre-internet, but these quotes seem far from contemporary. Paul's first quote came from the sixth century before Christ. The second citation was penned by Aratus around 280 B.C. Epimanides and Aratus hardly qualify as Athenian rock stars! Paul transports these poetic words some 600 and 300 years forward into his message. How hip would it be to quote America's first president, George Washington, to the guy at Starbucks? Or what about someone from the Dark

Ages? Granted, George Washington said and did a lot of remarkable things, but he's not exactly starring in any of this week's top five movies.

Paul used the first quote to say that life is all about God. Your bodily existence, the exercise of your mind, will, and emotions and your mental and spiritual existence *all* depend on God. All happens in *him*. You Athenians have assumed you are too important. You think you were raised from the ground of Greece. You think the world was made up of only Athenians and barbarians. But the real God is much bigger than you think!

4. God is the Father of Humanity.

> . . . as even some of your own poets have said,
> "For we are indeed his offspring."
>
> Being then God's offspring, we ought not
> to think that the divine being is like gold or
> silver or stone, an image formed by the art and
> imagination of man. (Acts 17:28b-29)

The second quote in verse 28 leads into Paul's fourth way of directing his hearers away from idolatry and toward the truth.

As we have seen, third century B.C. Stoic author Aratus, who was from Paul's native land of Cilicia, was the source of Paul's second *pop* quote. The glimmer of truth from Aratus that Paul makes to shine is about the nature of God. Greeks thought the divine nature was in man, but the Bible teaches that man is created by God, in God's image. Aratus was writing about Zeus. So, although he had stumbled onto some real truth about the nature of 'God,' it was incomplete and inadequate.[47]

In a general way, God can be said to be the father of all of his creatures. In a special sense, he is the adoptive father only of believers in Christ. It is this general sense, though, that Paul uses to make his point from the pagan poem. Since we are all God's offspring, we ought not to think the divine being is some kind of manmade invention.

We are derived from God and depend on God. It is ridiculous to think of the living God as a statue made of gold or silver, no matter how skillful or ingenious the artistry or how much the gold might be worth. A mere manmade monument could never represent humanity's Father God![48]

5. God will Judge the World.

> The times of ignorance God overlooked, but now he commands all people everywhere to repent, because he has fixed a day on which he will judge the world in righteousness by a man whom he has appointed; and of this he has given assurance to all by raising him from the dead. (Acts 17:30-31)

Wise Athenian ignorance is a theme Paul returns to. The times of ignorance were when the light of the revelation of God was confined to a single nation. Instead of shining God's light of blessing to the other nations, Israel hid it under a big basket. The rest of the world floundered in ignorance. As we have seen, however, the world was never in complete darkness.

The faint light of general revelation in creation, conscience, and provision (Acts 14:16, 17) was always shining. But in their sinfulness, the nations suppressed that light. Spiritual ignorance is never bliss because it is never innocent. The pagan superstitions and false religions being practiced this very moment all around the globe are not harmless. The participants in these empty religious activities are sinning against the one true God. They are guilty.

The fact that the former ignorance had to be "overlooked" confirms that it was guilty ignorance. "You Athenians," says Paul, "are guilty before God no matter how piously you may have acted without God."

"Overlooked" doesn't mean unnoticed or excused. Romans 3:25 states that God put Jesus "forward as a propitiation by his blood, to be received by faith. This was to show God's righteousness, because in his divine forbearance he had passed over former sins."

Acts 14:16, 17, Romans 3:25, and Acts 17 all indicate that the coming of Christ brought a fresh start in God's dealings with humanity.[49] The gospel of Christ launched from Israel to the nations, but now the nations are held to a higher standard of accountability. F. F. Bruce rightly concludes, "If ignorance of the divine nature was culpable before, it is inexcusable now."[50]

The call for repentance is universal. Not only do *all* people need to repent, but *all* people *everywhere*. The guilt of your ignorance will soon be called to account. Repent! Repentance is a change in a person's fundamental mindset or heart attitude which produces a change of lifestyle. In Athens, like Thessalonica, discarding idols would be evidence of real repentance ("you turned from idols to serve the living and true God," 1 Thessalonians1:9), but in both cases this call is not limited to idols. God requires a comprehensive change of heart and life.

There are three unchanging facts about the coming judgment in verse 31:

The coming judgment will be worldwide.

All people living when Jesus returns will qualify for judgment. All people who die at any time before Jesus returns also qualify for that judgment. Rich people and poor people will be judged. The tall and the small will be judged. The Judge will stare down at people of every hair color, eye color, and skin color. No exceptions will be made.

The coming judgment will be righteous.

There will be no possibility for any miscarriage of justice.[51] No slick lawyers will get guilty defendants off before this judge. This judgment will be a grand display of God's essential justice.

The coming judgment has been determined.

I don't know *what* day has been fixed, but I know *that* a day has been fixed. Every single day that passes moves us closer to the appointed day of judgment. As Kent Hughes puts it, "Mankind is not moving toward extinction (as Epicureans thought), nor toward absorption in the cosmos (as the Stoics thought). But mankind is moving [directly] toward divine judgment."[52]

Not only has the day been fixed, but the Judge has already been appointed. Who is this appointed judge?

> . . . God anointed Jesus of Nazareth with the
> Holy Spirit and with power. He went about
> doing good and healing all who were oppressed
> by the devil, for God was with him . . . And he

commanded us to preach to the people and to
testify that he is the one appointed by God to
be judge of the living and the dead. To him all
the prophets bear witness that everyone who
believes in him receives forgiveness of sins
through his name." (Acts 10:38, 42, 43)

"Truly, truly, I say to you, an hour is coming, and
is now here, when the dead will hear the voice
of the Son of God, and those who hear will live.
For as the Father has life in himself, so he has
granted the Son also to have life in himself. And
he has given him authority to execute judgment,
because he is the Son of Man. Do not marvel at
this, for an hour is coming when all who are in
the tombs will hear his voice and come out, those
who have done good to the resurrection of life,
and those who have done evil to the resurrection
of judgment. (John 5:25-29)

"All nations have been created from the first man,
Adam; through the last Adam, all nations will be judged."[53]
The visible validation of Jesus as judge came when he was
raised from the dead. The resurrection vindicated Jesus
and declared him to be both Lord and judge. As Paul said
in his message to the Athenians, God "has given assurance
to all by raising him from the dead."

Everything Jesus taught was confirmed by the
resurrection. Jesus was not just another well meaning

teacher, one who was sincere but sincerely wrong. He didn't merely die for a noble cause. Jesus Christ was literally, bodily raised from the dead on the third day. His message was right and his judgment is certain.

Here is Paul standing on center stage in the religious and intellectual capitol of the Roman Empire. No one there believes a person could rise from the dead. But does Paul engage his audience with a philosophical foundation for the plausibility of resurrection? No, he just says it. Instead of trying to *prove* that Jesus is alive, he *proclaims* that Jesus is alive and lets the Holy Spirit open the hearts of his hearers to the authenticity of his account. Then, after simply proclaiming it as fact, he audaciously uses the resurrection as *proof* of the judgment to come.

What Happens When We Upset Our World?

The historian records three reactions to the appeal of Paul's message—mockery, delay, and faith.

> Now when they heard of the resurrection of the dead, some mocked. But others said, "We will hear you again about this." So Paul went out from their midst. But some men joined   him and believed, among whom also were Dionysius the Areopagite and a woman named Damaris and others with them. (Acts 17: 32-34)

Mockery

The first edition of the report of a resurrection piqued the philosophers' desire for more (v. 19). The sequel, however, saw some of the audience demand their money back. Hearing the bold claim of resurrection itself, plus the fact that resurrection assures future judgment, caused the previously open gates of Areopagan interest to slam shut.

The hostility erupting in their hardened hearts did not smolder quietly. Mockery fired from the mouths of some of these "open-minded" fellows. Remember, to the Greek mind, our human bodies and all other things physical were considered evil. Only things spiritual were good. The idea of a bad body rising after the final freedom death brought was bizarre and offensive. Paul not only said just that, but he also used it as evidence that *their sins* would be called into account by that very risen person! Was this some kind of sick philosophical joke?

It may be significant that the Greek poet Aeschylus had depicted the god Apollo as denying the possibility of resurrection at the occasion of the inauguration of the Areopagus itself! "Once a man dies and the earth drinks up his blood, there is no resurrection."[54] This assumption may have fueled the meanness of the mockery toward Paul.

Delay

The fact that other hearers commented, "We will hear you again about this," could be taken as a polite dismissal. But coming on the heels of the previous reaction, these words seem more like a positive consideration of the gospel.[55] Aren't you thankful when you are not blasted away in hostile rejection as you share Christ with others? God is always sovereignly working through his word to accomplish all sorts of results. But as one who longs for a positive response to the good news, I appreciate it when a hearer seems to listen to the truth and give it honest consideration.

Faith

As this amazing showdown ends, Paul just leaves—meeting over. We might be tempted to think of this event as a failure, but it was not. Again, God is always working through our gospel interactions in far reaching ways that we may never realize in this lifetime. Paul did his job. He stepped up in the face of a hostile environment before an elite intellectual crowd and told the truth. He didn't give a pre-gospel "feel good" sermonette, hoping to get invited back next week. He didn't get lost in trying to out-philosophize the philosophers. He didn't leave out the offensive parts of the good news, like sin, judgment, and, in that culture, the resurrection itself. He said it all.

With an audience devoid of Old Testament foundations, Paul told them that God is the creator and sustainer of all life. He sought to resonate with their knowledge of general revelation. Paul alerted them to their accountability before the risen Judge, Jesus. He removed all potential excuses of ignorant idolatry. And the Athenians heard the call to repent before it was too late. The message may have included more than Luke's inspired summary, and certainly it was cut short by the audience. But isn't it amazing what Paul got to say? And isn't it amazing that he had the courage to say it? He was probably just getting over the painful reminders of his last beatings from a few months earlier.

With his job done, Paul leaves. But notice that he doesn't leave alone. Some men joined him and believed. One of the men and one prominent woman are mentioned by name. Can you imagine the ridicule and abuse that Dionysius the Areopagite must have faced? There is a cost to following Christ, and no doubt Dionysius had to make substantial payments immediately! Later tradition says that he became the first bishop of Athens.[56]

The woman's name was Damaris. Nothing else is known about her. This, however, is the third city mentioned on our journey through Acts 17, and the third indication of a prominent female convert (vv. 4, 12, 34)! In addition to these two, Luke tells us that there were "others with them."

The Athenians of today have tried to make up for the lack of response of their first century ancestors by engraving Paul's speech on a bronze tablet at the foot of the ascent to the Areopagus. They have also named a neighboring thoroughfare in honor of the Apostle.[57]

Conclusion

*From Being Upset about Evangelism
to Being a World Upsetter*

A FAILURE TO PLAN is a plan to fail. There is something to be gained from applying this familiar adage to upsetting our world. A great deal of passion for evangelism dissimilates into thin air for the want of a plan.

Passion for the Christ's glory to be spread fuels our witness. Glowing love for the Lord overcomes many fears of failure. Desire to obey the Great Commission encourages action. Knowing Gospel answers prepares us to respond to those asking questions.

These ingredients are essential, but are they adequate to upset your world?

Paul did not enter Thessalonica, Berea, and Athens with a pack of passion and mental preparation and then go about his business hoping some Gospel conversation might come along. Paul had a specific agenda for impact. He came into Macedonia and Greece with a plan—he entered the synagogue; he went to the marketplace.

Passion without a plan squanders opportunities for you to upset your world. Don't come to the end of our study only inspired by Paul's passion—determine to imitate his example, mapping out his mission. Take a few minutes to spell out action steps that will put you on the path to upsetting your world.

Where are the religious people in your world? Be very specific. What can you do this week to initiate a conversation with one or two of them? What two or three questions will you use to begin the conversation?

What literature do you want to have on hand to be able to leave with them? Does it need to be ordered? Does it need to be written?

What night can you make time to visit a bookstore for the purpose of engaging an inquiring mind? Is there a book for sale at the store that you can hold in your hand to use as a bridge to begin the engagement?

Do you have a desire to be a light in a Sunday School class at your local liberal church? Set up a time to discuss with your church leaders whether or not it is best for you to engage in this kind of evangelism. Let them guide you about the best way to do it.

Identify your intellectual world. What concrete steps can you establish right now that will create a conversation with one or two of them this week? What are their most likely concerns about Christ and the gospel? What preparation can you make to anticipate your response? Ask your leaders to suggest a good book for you to read on the subject.

Can you enroll in a college class next semester? What about an intensive class for a few hours each day for a week? Structuring your life to upset intellectuals with the message of Jesus takes some effort. Start right now. Choose the school. Begin the application process this week.

What do you see as you look at your schedule? Our calendars reveal our true priorities. A passionate sports fan creates time to watch the games, read the stories, and even works in time to argue with his friends about his or her favorite team. A passionate Christian should also calendar time to upset the world.

Focus your gospel zeal into a plan. Make an agenda for something that will have an eternal impact, sharing the good news of the Lord Jesus Christ. May the Lord be pleased to have it said of you and me, "These men who have upset the world have come here also!"

Acknowledgments

I AM SO THANKFUL for the mercy of God in sending the Lord Jesus to live perfectly and suffer and die for sinners like me! Without your mercy and grace there would be no gospel to proclaim to the world. Thank you for saving me and giving me the privilege of telling others of how great you are.

Thank you to Anna Maupin for being a great friend and a great editor. Your input always makes the message clearer! Thanks to Bill May, the firefighter writer, for your excellent suggestions. Thank you to Jim, Daryl, Benjamin, and Steve at CCW. Your belief in the project and your careful readings of the manuscript produced a better final product. It truly became a real team effort.

Thank you to Rick Kress for your eagerness to see this book in print. You have been a faithful friend since our time together in California. I am so glad the Lord is using you as both a pastor and a publisher. May the Lord get the message out far and wide for his glory!

Notes

1.   Jim Elliff is president of Christian Communicators Worldwide. These thoughts were expressed at a F.I.R.E conference in Sharpsburg, GA in 2005.

2.   cf. John Stott, *The Message of Acts* (Downers Grove, IL: IVP, 1990), 279, and I. Howard Marshall, Tyndale New Testament Commentaries: Acts (Grand Rapids, MI: Eerdmans Publishing Co., 1980), 276. I am indebted to many scholars for helping me understand and communicate the meaning of this glorious passage in its historical context. Although I have sought to cite all of my sources, it is possible some of their thoughts unintentionally made it into this book without notation. The most helpful commentaries I used were by John Stott, I. Howard Marshall , Homer Kent, F.F. Bruce, Kent Hughes, and John Polhill. The full citation of each of these works appears within the endnotes.

3.   cf. Acts 16:13; 17:10, 16-17; 18:1-4, 11, 19, 26; 19:8, 9.

4.   John MacArthur, *The MacArthur Study* Bible (Nashville, TN: Word Publishing), 1664.

5.   Sidney Greidanus, *Preaching Christ from the Old Testament* (Grand Rapids, MI: Eerdmans Publishing Co., 1999), 184.

6.   Stott, *The Message of Acts,* 271.

7.   J.A. Alexander, *Acts of the Apostles* (Edinburgh, Scotland: Banner of Truth Trust, reprinted 1991, originally published 1857), 136.

8.   Marshall, 278.

9.   A.T. Robertson, *Word Pictures in the New Testament, Volume III, The Acts of the Apostles* (Grand Rapids, MI: Baker Book House, reprinted from 1930), 270.

10.   John B. Polhill, *The New American Commentary: Acts* (Nashville, TN: Broadman Press, 1992), 361.

11.   Stott, *The Message of Acts*, 272, 273.

12.   F.F. Bruce, *The New International Commentary on the New Testament: The Book of Acts* (Grand Rapids, MI: Eerdmans Publishing Co., 1988), 321.

13.   Bruce, 325.

14.   Polhill, 362.

15.   See Kevin DeYoung and Ted Kluck, *Why We're Not Emergent (By Two Guys Who Should Be)* (Chicago, IL: Moody Press, 2008). On pages 177-178, nine characteristics of emerging churches are compared to the guiding principles of the Unitarian Universalist Association.

16.   Bruce, 227.

17.   Polhill, 363.

18.   Marshall, 280.

19.   Polhill, 363.

20.   Robertson, 274.

21. Stott, *The Message of Acts*, 274

22. Bruce, 329.

23. Stott, *The Message of Acts*, 276.

24. ibid., 277.

25. ibid.

26. ibid.

27. ibid., 278.

28. Cited by John Stott, 279-280, from Constance E. Padwick, *Henry Martyn, Confessor of the Faith* (IVF, 1953), 146.

29. ibid.

30. ibid., 281.

31. ibid., 280.

32. Marshall, 281.

33. ibid., 284.

34. Homer Kent, *Jerusalem to Rome: Studies in Acts* (Grand Rapids, MI: Baker Book House, 1972), 284.

35. Marshall, 284.

36. Kent, 139.

37. ibid.

38. See Bruce, 332.

39. Marshall, 286.

40. Kent, 140.

41. Stott, *The Message of Acts*, 285.

43. Bruce, 337.

44. see Marshall's discussion of interpretive options for this phrase, 288.

45. Marshall, 288

46. Stott, *The Message of Acts*, 286.

47. ibid.

48. Isaiah 44:9-20.

49. Bruce, 340.

50. ibid.

51. Stott, *The Message of Acts*, 288

52. Kent Hughes, *Acts: The Church Afire* (Wheaton, IL: Crossway Books, 1996), 234-235.

53. Stott, *The Message of Acts*, 288.

54. Bruce, 343.

55. Marshall, 291.

56. ibid.

57. Bruce, 344.